JOURNEY

David & Grace

Messiah Jesus

A Journey that Changed the World

Journey with Jesus!

Jim Bryden

O&U
Onwards & Upwards

Messiah Jesus

Onwards and Upwards Publishers

4 The Old Smithy, London Road, Rockbeare,
Exeter, EX5 2EA, United Kingdom.

www.onwardsandupwards.org

Copyright © Jim Bryden 2020

The right of Jim Bryden to be identified as the author of this work has been asserted by the author in accordance with the Copyright, Designs and Patents Act 1988. All rights reserved. No part of this publication may be reproduced or transmitted in any form or by any means, electronic or mechanical, including photocopy, recording or any information storage and retrieval system, without permission in writing from the author or publisher.

First edition, published in the United Kingdom by Onwards and Upwards Publishers (2020).

ISBN:	978-1-78815-706-3
Typeface:	Sabon LT
Editor:	Hilja Jeffery
Graphic design:	LM Graphic Design

The views and opinions expressed in this book are the author's own, and do not necessarily represent the views and opinions of Onwards and Upwards Publishers or its staff.

Endorsements

In *Messiah Jesus* Jim Bryden takes his reader on a journey of discovery: discovery of the man Jesus, who lived and walked in Palestine two thousand years ago; and discovery of the Lord Jesus, who lives and walks with his people today. He also gives us the opportunity to think deeply about how his life impacts on our lives, and about what we discover about ourselves through our encounter with him.

Jim brings scenes of Jesus' earthly life and ministry to life in 16 easily readable chapters with topics for discussion or reflection to help us assimilate the teaching in each. I commend this book to those who are seekers after the truth about Jesus and the truth about ourselves.

Lieut-Colonel Ian Barr, B.D., M.A
Salvation Army Officer in Retirement

'He who would valiant be 'gainst all disaster,
Let him in constancy follow the master.'
These words from John Bunyan's classic hymn sum up the theme of Jim Bryden's second invitation to join him on an exciting journey of faith. We are invited to reflect on key moments in the life and ministry of our Lord, and consider their impact on our own Christian living. Questions for reflection or discussion challenge our thinking and may inspire new spiritual insight.

Dr John Coutts M.A., B.D., Ph.D.
Formerly Senior Lecturer in Theology,
University of Greenwich

About the Author

As a young teenager and non-churchgoer, Jim had a Damascus Road encounter with Christ which was to lead him into ministry in The Salvation Army. He and his wife Helen were ordained and commissioned as officers in 1968 and served in Scotland, South America, Zimbabwe and England.

Always a pastor and preacher first, he's held a variety of posts as a tutor and lecturer in Bible studies and Theology at The Salvation Army's International College in London and as Training Principal in Zimbabwe.

Besides academic and pastoral responsibilities, for the last six years of active ministry he held the post of Territorial Ecumenical officer for the United Kingdom and Republic of Ireland.

He holds a Bachelor of Divinity degree (Glasgow) and a Masters in Systematic Theology from King's College London.

To Helen,
my darling wife,
and
our two children:

Sheron Kourosh
'Journeying with us'

David Bryden
1964-2009
'With the Lord'

Messiah Jesus

Contents

Messiah Jesus

Introduction

I INVITE YOU TO FOLLOW 'MESSIAH JESUS', GOD'S Son, who has changed the world. This journey of faith has been planned by God himself. The star is his only Son, Jesus. We are all God's treasured creation. Still, our genetic make-up causes us to run away from God, instinctively thinking this a better choice than to follow God's way. Try as we may, we can never put flight from God into reverse gear. Some would not want that anyway. As long as we choose to live as we decide and not as God offers, we could end up being eternally lost. We'll never know or see the glory God wills for us to have.

Put another way, should you choose to walk with Jesus, you will be led to heights and depths that will stagger your emotions, challenge your take on life and propel you to places you never for a moment dreamt were possible. In the journey of faith, recognition of Jesus' oneness with God, his love for the Father, and humanity's brokenness that cries out for healing, feature widely. The love of God expressed through his Son's teachings, how he lived, his death on the cross and resurrection, send the promise of life eternal to all who believe. Do you believe?

Whether you do or not, stay with the programme. It takes you back to significant historical events in which Jesus the Messiah is defined by serving and saving. He meets friend and foe just where they are and stretches out his hand of peace and power. He stands sentinel against the forces of darkness. He knows what it is to be tempted and to triumph. Depending on which side of the fence you stand, when you see him approaching, you will either stand back or run to meet him. At the end of the day, Jesus, the world-changer, the King of Kings and Lord of Lords, humbly, rode into Jerusalem on a donkey only after he wept sorely for God's people. He received a mixed reception. Some cheered, others jeered. Why not pace yourself and take time to read all of this journey that changed the world, opening yourself to see, to hear and follow Jesus' call? If you choose to follow where he leads, it will be nothing less than the greatest decision of your whole life now and in the life that is to come!

1

God Who Makes His Son Known

Matthew 16:13-20

"…You are the Messiah, the Son of the living God." Jesus replied, "You are blessed, Simon … my Father in heaven has revealed this to you…"

Matthew 16:16,17 (NLT)

WHO AM I? WHAT MAKES ME THE PERSON I AM? What do other people think of me? On our journey of faith, these are questions we wrestle with all our days. How people see us may be poles apart from how we view ourselves. Either way, there remains much misinformation and misperception. Eighteenth-century poet Robert Burns wrote:

O would some power the gift [give] us,
To see ourselves as others see us.

In a strictly personal and private meeting with his disciples, Jesus flags up more of the world's greatest questions. These are perfectly normal everyday questions people might put to each other. *What do people say about me? What do you think of me?* They connect with character and reputation. In the case of Jesus, much more

11

lay behind such questions. Jesus knew on earth his days were numbered. It was crucial that his disciples would grasp exactly who he was ahead of his departure.

Caesarea Philippi, the location where this incredible event took place, was a region steeped in the worship of multiple deities – hardly holy ground! Centuries before in a similar environment, King David proclaimed:

> *I will praise you, LORD, with all my heart;*
> *before the 'gods' I will sing your praise.*
>
> *Psalm 138:1 (NIVUK)*

Away from public scrutiny Jesus seeks feedback on the public mind of who he is, before inviting their personal perceptions and beliefs on the matter. Each is quite vocal. Popular opinion sees him as a great prophet from the recent or distant past.

'Who do you say I am?'[1] Jesus asks.

Only Peter speaks. The others may have had a faintish notion but Peter says, 'You're the Christ, the Messiah, the Son of the living God.'[2]

Had Peter of his own volition, his reasoning and searching, uncovered the greatest discovery in the world? No way! God alone empowered Peter to see the unique relationship of Jesus to himself. When at God's instigation this happens to a person, that individual is transformed beyond words.

Away from the crowd in small groups is often the place where even the shiest among us share our deepest thoughts. Behind closed doors many of the big issues of life

---

[1] Matthew 16:15 (NIVUK)
[2] Matthew 16:16 (MSG)

are thrashed out. Politics, education, medicine, law, social, scientific, personal and religious matters have both a public and a private face.

In society, it is hard to think of a place more personal than home. There things are said and done that are influenced by what happens in the public arena. More importantly, in our 'private space' the 'public face' matters less. We all see things and do things that are the peculiar to our own inner circle of life. Whatever else 'home sweet home' is, it is the place where those closest to us see us as we really are.

Swiftly in response to Peter's awesome confession of who Jesus is, Jesus now tells him who *he* is! He is the 'rock' on which the church will be built. What does Jesus mean here by the word 'rock'? This is a question that has dogged the people of God over the centuries. Is the rock referring to the truth of Jesus made known by God? Is the focus on faith where Jesus as God's Son is acknowledged as the foundation stone of the church? Or should we take it that Peter, the man, is himself the rock?

There is a real sense in which each of these suggestions mirror the reality that is before us. The Old Testament frequently refers to God himself as the rock:

> *And who is the Rock except our God?*
>
> *Psalm 18:31 (NIVUK)*

If, then, Peter is the rock, he is not so in the sense that he forms the foundation of the Church. God alone is the architect and Christ its foundation.[3] Peter is more like a

---

[3]   See 1 Peter 2:4-8; Ephesians 2:20-22

first stone, shaped by God, on which to build his Son's community of faith. He is the first, the first of many, who joyfully and eagerly proclaim what God alone has made known, namely, that Jesus Christ is Lord! The powers of death itself will be impotent against the body and the building up of God's people. Peter is indeed that foundation stone of God's new community brought into being by Christ and destined to live for ever. The apostle James would lead the Church in Jerusalem and the apostle Paul would emerge as God's special agent to non-Jews. All who surrender their life to Christ build on the solid rock of faith in him who cannot fall or fail. Whom are you building on?

Today our God has called each of us to himself. Ours is to follow in the trail of his people over the ages; to be what he wants us to be. We each are called into covenant and contracted to build his kingdom on earth, brick by brick.

Jesus further entrusts into Peter's keeping the 'keys of the kingdom of Heaven'[4]. He will be given authority that has eternal implications for the Church of God. A good example of this is the principal role he played in the early Church. He proclaimed the door of the kingdom as wide open to Jews, proselytes and Gentiles.[5]

Today, we who confess 'Jesus is Lord' are commissioned to reach those with little or no appetite for the things of God. Tragically, hunger for the things of God has all but disappeared from our society as more and more

---

[4] Matthew 16:19 (NIVUK)
[5] See Acts 2

feed on a diet of self-advancement and an exclusively rationalistic, secular and scientific understanding of life, in which God no longer fits the equation. Ours is a rescue mission. Oh, that they may see Jesus!

Peter's onerous responsibility for deciding upon the life and mission of God's community will not be Peter-driven, but heaven-directed. None of us, not even Peter, is in charge of God's affairs. At best we are trusted stewards and servants, never overlords. Ours is the task to tend and guard the flock of God's people; but it is God alone who reigns supreme. Together, as one in Christ, may God's own Holy Spirit open our eyes to see, as we have never seen before, he who is the one and only Son of the living God!

QUESTIONS

Is it required of those who follow Christ to share their faith? If so, how? If not, why?

_____

_____

_____

_____

We all like to be valued and well thought of in life. Does it matter what family and community think of us?

_____

_____

_____

_____

How do you go about creating a need and hunger for those in society today who have settled for self-promotion and pride?

_____

_____

_____

_____

2

The Love of God

John 10:11-18; Acts 4:8-12; 1 John 3:1-2

How great is the love the Father has lavished on us, that we should be called children of God! And that is what we are!

1 John 3:1 (NIVUK)

WHILE WRITING THIS CHAPTER I HEARD THE voices of my wife and daughter expressing deep concern over the fact that we live in a 'broken world'. Don't we all know it! Even the best of human effort to make things better is flawed from the start. Many have strayed like sheep from God's fold. They have settled for 'my take on life'. God doesn't figure. They have no desire to be in God's family. It is hardly surprising the world is in such a state!

As we traverse along this journey of faith, I invite you to look at Jesus as shepherd, Peter's courageous speech and John's gripping description of the children of God.

In Jesus' account of the Good Shepherd, the sheep matter above everything else. When they get lost or are in danger, no sacrifice is too great in the search to find and save, death included. The shepherd's relationship to the flock is undergirded by a trust and protection clause. He's sensitive to their cries for help and quick to attack any who

17

pose a threat to their safety and survival. A strong bond exists between shepherd and sheep. They know his voice. They follow him. The hired hand, shepherding for the money, couldn't care less for the sheep. At the first sign of danger, he takes to his heels, leaving the flock to be devoured by wolves.

In these days when many make fame, fortune and finance the driving force of their lives, families and communities get divided and broken. For God's people, the call to be different, protect the vulnerable, reach out to the abused, fight for justice and share the good news of hope in Christ as shepherd requires that we recognise his voice and follow where he leads.

The thrust of Jesus' teaching is testimony to his relationship to the Father, what he does for him and his people, both those who already are and those who will be one with the Father, even as he is! For this to happen, the price is beyond measure. The Son will lay down his life. It is an act, more than any other, that shows us the amazing love of God.

Who would have thought the healing of a severely disabled man involving Peter and John could cause such a furore among the ruling authorities? When the disciples are hauled before the nation's leaders after a night in jail, these leaders display all the signs that they have the upper hand. Assembled are the top brass, an indication of how worried they are. The real reason for the arrest and trial of the disciples was their preaching and promotion of Jesus. Who is on trial? It is supposed to be Peter and John. Peter, however, in the power of the Holy Spirit, doesn't mince his words. With incredible boldness, he accuses them of rejecting and killing Jesus, but 'God raised [him] from the dead'[6]. The one they disregarded like a stone is the very foundation and exclusive channel of God's salvation for the world.

Are we ready and able to take our stand for Christ? Do we shudder at the challenge to speak up for him? Have we become so tamed, so condition by political correctness, that we tremble in our shoes to take on, should faith demand it, the leading lights of society? Only in the power of the Holy Spirit can we do it.

The Olympic Games are the place for the world's leading sports competitors to compete and strive for the top prize. The apostle John lights the Olympic flame for the prize greater than any other. It is to see Christ and be like him!

John races with breathtaking speed to share the prized trophy of God's amazing love and grace. The winners know they are 'children of God'[7], not in name only but in reality. They have been born again! How can this be? God made it happen. His abundant love has been lavished on them. They didn't bring it about. They couldn't.

As children of God we have received his life. We're not the people we were. We now have a new identity. It is this 'new you' that puzzles the world. We really have been made different. We may look the same but we think and act differently. Our choice of lifestyle, our standards, our perspective on life and people, is directed by God's Holy Spirit. He's the one who brings about the change, not us.

---

[6] Acts 4:10 (NIVUK)
[7] 1 John 3:1 (NIVUK)

We're no longer free to 'do our own thing'. If this sounds like bondage, spoilsport stuff, it's anything but. As God's children we prize, above all, knowing and doing his will.

How well I remember as a young teenager coming into faith in Christ. The change God made in my life was utterly amazing and my eyes searched for the path God set out for me. One Christian gentleman told me, 'Follow God's will.' It was a cold winter's day. There was no central heating in our home and in the lounge the coal fire blazed with a red glow. In the kitchen the potatoes and vegetables were on the boil and steam spread like thick mist into the stairwell. I stood on the landing and with my index finger wrote on the steamed glass window, 'To know and do the will of God.' This inspired desire has remained with me all my life.

Together let us, as one, follow Christ wherever he leads, not counting the cost, secure in the knowledge that we who were lost are now found; we who shrunk from daring have been made courageous; we who were orphans have been chosen and adopted into God's family. By his Spirit we are to be like our Lord and are guaranteed one day to see him as he really is!

QUESTIONS

Should following Christ require you to place your life in danger as Jesus taught in the parable of The Good Shepherd? If no, explain why. If yes, what practical and spiritual equipment would be priority?

Present a case for the uniqueness of Christianity as the *only* way of salvation as proclaimed by Peter in Acts 4:11,12.

The believer is lavished with God's love, chosen to be *like* Jesus and is earmarked one day to see him. What impact does this truth have on our everyday lives? (Read 1 John 3:1-3.)

3

Journey of Discovery

Matthew 16:13-28; Daniel 7:13,14

Then Jesus said to his followers, "If any of you want to be my follower, you must stop thinking about yourself and what you want. You must be willing to carry the cross that is given to you for following me."

Matthew 16:24 (ERV)

FOR MANY PEOPLE LIFE IS A JOURNEY OF DIS-covery about who they are. The ancient Greek saying, 'Know thyself,' was based on the assumption that the better we know ourselves, the better we will understand other people. The most wonderful reality is knowing Jesus! When we know him, we truly know ourselves and can best relate to others.

In Matthew 16:13-28, the disciples made the most incredible journey of discovery about themselves and their master, Jesus. Crowds had come to see and hear this captivating young rabbi. They had seen miracles of healing of broken bodies, scarred minds and darkened souls. The man from Nazareth, who said to certain fishermen,

'Come, follow me ... and I will send you out to fish for people,'[8] was like no one else they had ever known.

The private meeting between Jesus and his disciples took place at Caesarea Philippi, near the base of Mount Hermon. This was Gentile territory where history and culture were thick with pagan worship, from Baal to the Greek god Pan. The secure sunshine of Galilean ministry was eclipsed by the clouds of uncertainty in what lay ahead. The wind of change was sounding. The shadows were gathering. Calvary's course was set. Jesus was ready, but were the disciples?

What question in the world matters more than any other? Is it about politics, philosophy or science? Does it relate to the origin of humankind and the world in which you live? No. It is quite simply, who is Jesus?

As we saw in chapter 1, Jesus needed to know if his disciples had grasped his true identity. He often referred to himself as the Son of Man, a term they would be familiar with.[9] So he asked the starter question: 'Who do people say the Son of Man is?' Public opinion regarded Jesus as one of the 'greats' come back to life: John the Baptist, Elijah or Jeremiah.[10] Some saw this 'greatness' in political terms, where the use of violence was legitimate towards the enemies of Jewry. This was not the way of Jesus.

Our journey of discovery now moves to its unrivalled answer – from public conception to private insight, close up and personal: 'But what about you?'

---

[8] Matthew 4:19 (NIVUK)
[9] See Daniel 7:13,14
[10] See Matthew 16:13,14

In 1972 I arrived in Peru with my wife and our two small children, David and Sheron. We were there as missionaries. The place felt all very new and strange. On that first night, tucking our frightened infant daughter into bed, her mum whispered reassuringly, 'Don't be frightened, darling. The Lord Jesus is here.' Eyes bright and wide, little Sheron protested, 'I'd rather have someone with skin on!'

But on that day at Caesarea Philippi, Peter knew that Jesus was God before him. He had Jesus with skin on!

The greatest question on earth remains: who is Jesus? No one outside God's enabling power possesses the capacity to understand, let alone know, the true and unique divinity of Christ. At best they may applaud him as a Gandhi, Martin Luther, Mother Teresa, a prophet – but that's as far as it goes. Why is this? Again, we find the answer from Jesus' own lips, where in response to Peter's recognition that he (Jesus) was Son of God he said:

> *"God bless you, Simon, son of Jonah! You didn't get that answer out of books or from teachers. My Father in heaven, God himself, let you in on this secret of who I really am."*
>
> *Matthew 16:17 (MSG)*

Only God can make God known. Other monotheistic faiths such as Islam and Judaism refuse to acknowledge Christ as God. Christians stand by the words of Jesus that God himself confirms the divinity of his Son,[11] therefore

---

[11] Luke 9:35

God is Father, God is Son and God is Holy Spirit, and though distinct, they are *one*.

Who do *you* say Jesus is?

QUESTIONS

In your journey of faith in Christ, what discoveries have you made of who he is and what he requires of those who would follow after him?

_____

_____

_____

What does Daniel 7:13,14 say to you about the relationship between the Ancient of Days and Son of Man and what was bestowed on him?

_____

_____

_____

Notice how Jesus and his disciples ministered in Gentile territory where pagan worship was widespread. What lessons does this hold for the Church today in respect of pagan practices?

_____

_____

_____

_____

4

The Best Will in the World

Matthew 16:21-26

"…Anyone who intends to come with me has to let me lead. You're not in the driver's seat; I am … Follow me and I'll show you how."

Matthew 16:24-25 (MSG)

OUR JOURNEY OF DISCOVERY ABOUT JESUS Christ becomes an inside-out exploration of our very selves. What we find is not always welcome. Our noblest intentions, however sincere or well-meaning, are not necessarily what please God. Only walking with Jesus – going where he leads and doing what he demands – will bring us into the pleasure and will of God and give us deep peace.

Let's now look at the cost of following Jesus, but also the fact that no matter the price we may have to pay, we can rest in the knowledge that God's mighty hand will hold us secure and guide us through the valleys of diversions or devilish temptations.

Jesus knew he must go forward to face immeasurable suffering and death, and told his disciples so. Peter protested, 'Never, Lord! ... This shall never happen to you!'[12]

The biting retort is not what we expect: 'Peter, get out of the way. Satan, get lost. You have no idea how God works.'[13]

One moment Peter is highly commended, the next, severely reprimanded. He got it right about the person and identity of Jesus, then got it wrong about his mission. With the best will in the world, he meant well. But he overstepped the mark and was used by Satan to tempt Jesus not to go through with God's will.

Life is like that. Sometimes we get it right, sometimes we don't. We insist on seeing things from our perspective. When our hearts are open to God, he will guide us to see what is hidden. When we fall back on our own ideas, coloured by our own desires – however unselfish or sophisticated – we reach conclusions that are simply human; but when we open lives to the beautiful, deepening work of God's Spirit, heavenly wisdom is imparted.

'All the best!' We love to be on the receiving end of such a greeting. Who would ever imagine 'the best' could have anything to do with sidelining ourselves? It's time to move from 'What's in it for me?' to 'What must I be prepared to give up as a mark of my devotion to Christ, who gave up everything for me?'

The disciples could not have been comfortable with the prospect of saying no to themselves and yes to a cross-like life in order to follow the master.[14] Once when I was

---

[12] Matthew 16:22 (NIVUK)
[13] Matthew 16:23 (MSG)
[14] See Matthew 16:24-26

passing through London Bridge railway station, I was confronted by a giant advertisement featuring Christian evangelists. They promised miracles and healing. But where, I could not help thinking, was mentioned the cost of discipleship? If the message looks only at personal comfort, it fails to speak the full gospel of Christ.

The truth is, we don't want to hear that the journey of discovery takes us to valleys of suffering or steep ascents that must be climbed. At all costs we must not set ourselves up as those who promote 'name it, claim it' or expect a God-insurance that offers protection from every storm.

All who follow Christ must carry a cross. This does not sit comfortably with today's 'give me' culture – inside and outside the Church. One hymn hardly sung now held a jewel of faith with the words, 'Take up thy cross and follow me … how can I make a lesser sacrifice, when Jesus gave his all?'[15] In society today there's an appetite for an easy, comfortable lifestyle. Such can be all-consuming. It's easy to celebrate our faith, but less attractive to live with the cross-cost.

But the truth is, those who follow Jesus are no longer in charge. Only Christ may sit in the driver's seat. He will take us into bandit country. We never know when the enemy will strike. He will not take a shortcut through peaceful valleys to reach the goal that calls for absolute sacrifice.

We'll get there. Yes, there will be peace in the valley, but it is Christ's peace of conquest: 'Peace I leave with you;

---

[15] *Take Up Thy Cross;* Alfred Henry Ackley (1887-1960)

my peace I give you.'[16] We'll reach our destination, but on God's terms. His will, his way, his power will be meat and drink to our souls. This is the greatest discovery of all. If we have peace and love, it is because we follow Jesus.

In these times of rapid and disturbing changes we must be ready to make that further journey into Christ – following his example by the power of his Spirit to give and not to count the cost. Jesus says, 'If any of you wants to be my follower, you must give up your own way, take up your cross daily, and follow me.'[17]

The journey into God is through the cross of Christ. Evangelist Dr Billy Graham went to the heart of the matter: 'Take me to the cross. I can find my way home from there!'

Fifty years ago I stood with other students for Christian ministry, ready to engage upon an incredible journey – armed with faith in God and equipped with his power, ready to go out into the world. We sang, 'Where he leads me, I will follow. I'll go with him, with him, all the way.'[18] Do that, and you have truly launched upon life's greatest journey of discovery. It starts and finishes with knowing the Christ of the cross. That way, we fathom our deepest selves, feel into Christ's compassion for others and, at the end, bring glory to God.

---

[16] John 14:27 (NIVUK)
[17] Matthew 16:24 (NIVUK)
[18] Luke 9:23 (NLT)

QUESTIONS

What do you think of the Christian's cross-centred life?

How crucial is it for the believer to make a total surrender of his/her will to the will of God?

List the treasures you have from following Jesus and the losses, were you not to do so.

5

Following or Failing
the Good Shepherd

Matthew 16:27,28; John 10:22-30

*"My sheep listen to my voice; I know them, and
they follow me."*

John 10:27 (NLT)

A FEW YEARS BACK MY WIFE AND I WERE TRA-
velling home from the borders of Scotland. We were going
through some beautiful scenic countryside when we passed
fields where sheep were grazing. Suddenly they began to
run and we wondered where they were going. It seemed
that they were going in every direction and actually not
making any headway.

I looked for a sheepdog who would prod and drive the
herd where they were meant to go. There was no sign of a
dog anywhere, so the sheep just seemed to go around in
circles, busy going nowhere. Had the shepherd been there,
it would have been such a different scenario. You see,
sheep will follow the shepherd for they know his voice and
trust him implicitly. The shepherd knows each animal
individually, because he cares for them and they somehow
know that. When he calls, they recognise the voice and
follow in the direction given.

In John's Gospel, we glimpse Jesus in winter weather, walking in the Temple precincts pursued by Jews whose pride is punctured and, but for a few, are resolved to 'take this man out' who has dared to challenge their authority and lay claim to a unique relationship with God. Some regard Jesus as raving mad, demon-possessed. A few are not so sure. When they witnessed Jesus give sight to a blind man, some said, 'Can a "maniac" open blind eyes?'[19]

The Jews ask Jesus, 'How long will you keep us in suspense? If you are the Christ, tell us plainly.'[20] Some genuinely want to know the truth. Most don't. The question is a plot to trap Jesus into a statement that could be twisted into a charge of blasphemy in a Jewish court or insurrection before the Roman governor. Still, Jesus responds. He notes that, first, they have disregarded his miracles that testify to God's approval. Next, they refuse to believe; in fact, they can't believe as they are not God's chosen. 'My sheep listen to my voice,' says Jesus. 'I know them, and they follow me.'[21]

Three things stand out in this passage: hearing, knowing and following.

In life there are many voices but only one that matters: the voice of the Good Shepherd. Tragically, when it comes to tuning into what's best for people in our global world, those other voices drown out the one that really counts. The Jews in the Temple who harassed and hounded Jesus were too full of themselves, too engrossed in their take on

---

[19] John 10:21 (MSG)
[20] John 10:24 (NIVUK)
[21] John 10:27 (NIVUK)

life and religion, to make any room for the man from Nazareth.

In Britain today, there is not only a falling away from God, many are blind as to where or how he should figure in their lives at all. In short, they don't give him a second thought unless faced with a catastrophe of alarming magnitude such as the death of a loved one, financial crisis, divorce, personal health breakdown, etc.

For others it is even worse; if they're not at war with God, they pour scorn on the claim that he exists. The outcome of such an approach to life carries with it serious consequences both for this life and the life to come. Tragically, many such people think they know best and insist upon finding their own way in life. The voices of pride and prejudice, secularism and sectarianism conquer and enslave. They are spiritually deaf and dead. On this score Jesus issued a stern warning in respect of the belief system adopted by the Jews who insisted they and they alone were right about their take on life and religion. He told them, 'For judgment I have come into this world, so that the blind will see and those who see will become blind.'[22] Christ needs to be heard. Only he has the answer. Only he can speak the words of life eternal.

Our beliefs help shape the kind of people we are. Our identity is defined by what and in whom we believe. We can't get away from the fact that faith in the things of God is not something that comes naturally. It is something imparted to us as a gift by God's Holy Spirit. The apostle Paul says, 'For it is by grace you have been saved, through

---

[22] John 9:39 (NIVUK)

faith – and this is not from yourselves, it is the gift of God.'[23] Daniel Webster's hymn puts it this way:

> *I know not how the Spirit moves,*
> *convincing men of sin;*
> *revealing Jesus through the Word*
> *creating faith in him.*

Believers don't know why they've been chosen but they know in whom they believe, and pay close attention to the voice of the Good Shepherd who generates his very own life within them: life eternal! What's more, that life of God remains even in the face of personal failure and satanic attack. The darkest hour, the deepest suffering, the questioning, the doubts, losing one's way like a wandering sheep – none of these will sever God's own from his mighty and saving hand. This is the promise of the Good Shepherd. What a belief, what an end!

If you follow Christ, you're hanging on his every word, in intimate relationship with him and, whatever the cost, are prepared to go where he leads, all the way! Those who fail to follow Christ suffer from spiritual deafness, a broken relationship, and pursue a personal agenda that is alien and destructive.

Don't be trapped into pursuing your own agenda, running aimlessly like the sheep in that Scottish field. It doesn't have to be that way. Listen to the call of Christ to life in all its fullness, where you know him intimately and follow him all the way.

---

[23] Ephesians 2:8 (NIVUK)

QUESTIONS

Why do you think so many in today's society have given up on God altogether or don't take him seriously?

_____

_____

_____

You are asked to present a portfolio of Jesus the Good Shepherd. What factors and truths would be at the top of your list?

_____

_____

_____

In his day Jesus had to deal with bitter opposition and hatred from many religious leaders. Why was this, how did Jesus deal with it and what does it say to us today?

_____

_____

_____

_____

6

Two Kinds of Peace

John 14:27; Philippians 4:7

"I am leaving you with a gift – peace of mind and heart. And the peace I give is a gift the world cannot give. So don't be troubled or afraid."

John 14:27 (NLT)

A FAMILY AT WAR WAS A TV DRAMA SERIES TELE-vised in the 1970s in Britain. Set in the Second World War, it lived up to its name as it focused on strains, tensions and broken relationships exacerbated by the war. Today it is a known fact that modern man is engaged in more conflict than ever before in human history. Even if the nations of the world were to unite and turn their 'swords into ploughshares'[24] and our shores became havens of peace, there would still be families at war.

When Jesus tutored his disciples on peace, he knew full well there was more to it than settling matters with the Roman occupying force. The disciples were gripped with panic. The thought of Jesus 'going away' had punched the stomach out of them. Distress and despair were written on their faces. But the gloom of uncertainty vanished when

---

[24] Isaiah 2:4 (NIVUK)

the Lord spoke with promise of peace. God's own Holy Spirit would echo Jesus' words and take them on a journey deeper into the heart and mystery of God himself!

There are two kinds of peace: the peace that at best is the absence of armed conflict of the battlefield and where family and community tensions are reduced to a bearable minimum. Then there's peace from God that, even though living and wrestling with the struggles of everyday life with its pain, its trauma, its challenges, we can share in the peace of God the Father, Son and Spirit!

Today Jesus offers us the peace the world cannot give. Like those early disciples, we can know we're not alone. Whatever lies before us, wherever we find ourselves, whoever may oppose us, if we look to Christ, we have his promise:

> *'I am leaving you with a gift – peace of mind and heart! And the peace I give isn't fragile like the peace the world gives. So don't be troubled or afraid.'*
>
> *John 14:27 (TLB)*

That old chorus testifies to it:

> *O the peace my Saviour gives.*
> *Peace I never knew before!*
> *And my way has brighter grown*
> *Since I learned to trust him more.*

I encourage you to dig a little deeper into this subject by reading Numbers 6:26, Psalm 85:8 and Colossians 3:15. Walk the path of God's rich blessings and peace to you in these verses!

QUESTIONS

'The peace of God, which transcends all understanding, will guard your hearts and minds in Christ Jesus.'[25] How does this truth resonate with your life?

How do you distinguish between the world's peace and God's peace?

Today many families are at war. What practical and spiritual service can the Church bring to promote peace at home?

---

[25] Philippians 4:7 (NIVUK)

7

The Power of God Then and Now

John 14:6; Ephesians 1:19b-23; Acts 1:4b

> *That power is the same as the mighty strength he [God] exerted when he raised Christ from the dead and seated him at his right hand in the heavenly realms...*
>
> *Ephesians 1:19,20 (NIVUK)*

CHRIST ALONE IS 'THE WAY, THE TRUTH AND the life'[26]. Where does this leave other faiths? Who knows, but God alone? This much is sure: if the others 'get there in the end', it's not that they have circumvented God's only way. At best, they traverse by a circuitous route that ultimately bows the knee in recognition that Christ alone is the only way to God. Only he has been given unique authority over all things.[27]

The world's perception of power at its simplest is 'the power to do anything'. This is broadly observable in nature, science, politics, the Church and in many management structures: power in the right hands can do a great deal of good; in the wrong hands we have abusers, exploiters and tyrants.

---

[26] John 14:6 (NIVUK)
[27] See Ephesians 1:19b-23

The path of history is strewn with the legacy of tyrants. The world we now live in is 'knee-deep' in trouble where people take power – the abuser in the home, the criminal in the street, the secret lover, the stranger to the truth and the trampling on the heads of others to 'get on'. Each of these are disregarding the precious freedoms and dignity of human beings, made as they are in the very image of God.

There is another power, the power that Jesus told his disciples to wait for, pray for and yearn for. It is the power from on high, that power of the Holy Spirit. At its heart is the love of God. Where people take God out of the equation, they are left with 'me power'. In the end, it leads only to wreck and ruin. The power that saves the world, and you and me, is not natural. It is not innate or automatic. It cannot be acquired even by the most disciplined moral standards. Meditation, philosophy or science cannot deliver on it. It is, as Jesus said, a gift from God.[28] This alone is the power that will make all things new: new people, new relationships and a new world.

---

[28] See Acts 1:4b

QUESTIONS

Jesus said, 'I am the way and the truth and the life. No one comes to the Father [God] except through me.' What does this tell us of his relationship with God? Where do you think this places Christianity in relation to other faiths?

_____

_____

_____

Where the use of power in communities and nations has a negative or even a destructive impact on peoples, what should the Church do?

_____

_____

_____

_____

Why do you think the 'power' of the Holy Spirit is needed in the life of the believer?

_____

_____

_____

_____

8

The Incredible Journey

Luke 19:28-44; Numbers 6: 26; Psalm 85:8; Colossians 3:15

> *'Blessed is the king who comes in the name of the Lord!' 'Peace in heaven and glory in the highest! ... 'If you, even you, [Jerusalem] had only known on this day what would bring you peace – but now it is hidden from your eyes.'*
>
> *Luke 19:38,42 (NIVUK)*

JUST DAYS BEFORE HIS CRUCIFIXION JESUS TRA-velled a road which at first was strewn with popularity and praise. Like all fame, it soon fades and takes its toll. That said, Jesus was not, as we shall see, blinded by the cheers of adoring fans. How well he knew that ahead stood a cross where the Son of God would suffer and die for the sins of the whole world. But still, he went forward.

The journey to Jerusalem that Jesus made in the literal sense had nothing unusual about it. He had been there before and knew the terrain and the people well. What made this particular journey incredible was that no one before or since has travelled the road Jesus took. He is our best dream come true. People and creation rise to meet him. Enemies fall at his feet. Heaven and earth sing at his coming. Light, life and love are his crown. Like no other, he alone is the way, the truth and the life!

Jesus' triumphal entry into Jerusalem, recorded by all four Gospels, is a measure of how significant it was. His mind was set on fulfilling the prophecy in Zechariah 9:9:

> *Rejoice greatly, Daughter Zion! Shout, Daughter Jerusalem! See, your king comes to you, righteous and victorious, lowly and riding on a donkey.*[29]

What? A *donkey?* The 'bringer of salvation to the whole world' on a donkey? The future King of Judah... The King of Kings... Here he comes, as someone said, 'not with swashbuckling bravado nor a prancing war horse' but in humility on the back of – a donkey!

Think of his mother over thirty years before, heavily pregnant, more than likely riding on a donkey for some ninety miles, the distance between Nazareth and Bethlehem – a journey of some four to five days.[30] After giving birth, she, Joseph and baby Jesus found themselves as wanton refugees fleeing the brutality of King Herod, who ordered the murder of every little boy two years and under living in Bethlehem and its surrounding area.[31]

Now this incredible journey winds its way into the heart of the chosen people of God where the authorities (who should have known better) have targeted him not as Messiah but a wanted man with a price on his head!

With his disciples Jesus passed through the villages of Bethany and Bethphage – only a few miles from Jerusalem. The group approached the city from the Mount of Olives

---

[29] NIVUK
[30] See Luke 2:4,5
[31] Matthew 2:13-15

and suddenly, like a glittering jewel, they saw the Temple. By now the crowds had gathered to give him a royal welcome. They had heard his teaching, witnessed his miracles and a number had followed his call. There was no holding back their level of enthusiasm:

> *"Blessed is he who comes,*
> *the King in God's name!*
> *All's well in heaven!*
> *Glory in the high places!"*
>
> *Luke 19:38 (MSG)*

It all got a bit much, perhaps embarrassing for some Pharisees who told Jesus to calm the crowd, bring them under control. One can just see an excited Jesus and hear his arresting response:

> *"If they keep quiet, the stones would do it for them, shouting praise."*
>
> *Luke 19:40 (MSG)*

What now lay ahead for this man from God? Where lay the future of the people of God? My, what a journey! Can you imagine the hush and the startled faces when in stark contrast, Jesus, on seeing Jerusalem, burst into tears! He knew then even before his rejection by the people and crucifixion that they were blind and deaf to God's visitation. We have here a lament that was crushing. *He saw, he wept, he pleaded.* How ironic the city of 'peace' is heading for ruin.

> *"If you had only recognised this day, and everything that was good for you! But now it's too late. In the days ahead your enemies are*

*going to bring up their heavy artillery and
surround you, pressing in from every side.
They'll smash you and your babies on the
pavement. Not one stone will be left intact. All
this because you didn't recognise and welcome
God's personal visit."*

Luke 19:41-44 (MSG)

Dr John Stott describes movingly for us a Jesus who,
on approaching Jerusalem with words of severe warning
and judgement on her, does so with tears of love. The God
who judges also weeps for his people. He does not will that
any should perish.

On this incredible journey, let's take time to look at the
people who gathered to see Jesus, the disciples who
followed him, the officials who opposed him, and ask,
what does this have to say to us today?

They were a strong mixture from many walks of life.
Some welcomed Jesus as the prophet from Galilee. Others
were moved by the miracles they witnessed. Then there
were those who were astounded and challenged by his
teaching. In short, in the crowd were fishermen, farmers,
the educated and the elite.

Today we are witnessing a flight *from* God and a
society in pursuit of fame, fortune and fans, be they pop
stars, footballers or TV entertainers; not here much
welcome to Jesus by those who reach for the white
dazzling stallion of glitter and stardom, where he is not on
the radar.

More and more have turned away from the 'welcoming
crowd' and prefer to chase after 'what's in life for me'.
Granted, there are a lot of 'good' people who do good

things for others but feel that the Christian Church has a cheek where it seeks to bring God into the equation of the spiritual aspect of life.

We're living in a time when the Humanist Society is having a field day. Numbers recruited to this optional form of spirituality are rising dramatically.

At a funeral I took recently I spoke with one of the funeral directors about the types of funerals that take place. He confirmed that more and more people are opting for a humanist funeral. These developments have to be a source of deep concern where people cut themselves off from God, the 'Giver of Life' himself!

The Scottish Parliament are currently faced with more and more humanists demanding their rights of life without God. It was Francis Schaeffer who said:

> *Humanism, man beginning only from himself, had destroyed the old basis of values, and could find no way to generate with certainty any new values. In the resulting vacuum the impoverished values of personal peace and affluence had come to stand supreme.*[32]

We have on our hands a big challenge as we travel the incredible journey of faith. We must guard against complacency, be armed with courage and pray in the power of the Spirit for the lost!

Some joined the disciple band and saw Jesus in purely political terms. Judas thought to force the hand of Jesus to use violence as a weapon of freedom from Roman

---

[32] *Great Quotes & Illustrations;* compiled by George Sweeting; Word Publishing (1987)

occupation. It backfired! We can never shape Jesus according to our personal ambitions. If you want to make the incredible journey and stay with the programme, you cannot at any time have things done 'your way'. There's only one way, as there's only one Lord and God. You can only stay the course if you follow Jesus!

Then there were those disciples who thought more of themselves than they did of the others: a special place in the kingdom of God – super! But Jesus taught:

> *'Whoever is the least among you is the greatest.'*
>
> Luke 9:48 (NLT)

There it is: push for stardom and look to be noticed, admired, envied for your talent, race after money, power and in kingdom values you are at the bottom of the pile. By contrast, the one who gladly stands back that others may be valued and supported has a greatness they don't know they have.

Some pressed for the crowds to be calmed for fear of rivalry, revolution and rebellion. Others promoted protective status, influence and power. All failed to recognise the Messiah when he came. What is it that makes people blind and deaf to God? In a word it is sin. What, you may ask, is sin? At its simplest, sin is doing 'our own thing' in life and not what God wills. We are made *by* God *for* God. To think and act otherwise creates a breach in the relationship between him and us which, if not put right, will lead to our destruction. How are things put right? It's something we can't do but God does.

So, do we leave it all to him? Yes or no?

Yes. By sending his only Son Jesus to die on the cross, God has provided the means of freeing us from ourselves. If not freed, we'd die and stay as good as dead without end.

No. God does not force the issue on us. If, however, we freely respond to his love and mercy received through his Son's death and resurrection, God grants us life in himself now and through all eternity.

In tracing this incredible journey, we witness Jesus confronting the enemy of God on their own ground: he healed the sick, fed the hungry, lifted the oppressed and cast out demons.

Today, many do not take the reality of Satan seriously. The apostle Peter paints him in this manner:

> *Be alert and sober minded. Your enemy the devil prowls around like a roaring lion looking for someone to devour.*
>
> *1 Peter 5:8 (NIVUK)*

Sometimes Satan comes with the sweet voice of reason, as he did when, following the glory of baptism, Jesus found himself in the blistering heat of the desert, wrestling with the shape his mission should take and how best to reach people with the treasures of God's kingdom.

Often after the highs there comes the lows. After a prolonged period of fasting, the devil suggests to Jesus that it's vital he eats. No food? Not a problem: as God's Son, turn the stones into bread. Feed the hungry. Give awe to your mission: jump from the top of the Temple's highest point, be a star performer. Show your power on a global scale; kneel to the tempter and all of earth's treasures will fall into your lap. Go on, go for it. Such is the cunning and conniving of the Evil One. His promise is pure poison, deadly when taken. Satan always looks for a way in which to end our incredible journey to God. His time is limited. He is a defeated foe. No one can stand against Christ who always overcomes. We're on the winning side when we keep our eyes on Christ. Christ alone will win!

This incredible journey in another sense started before the beginning of time. It was always in the heart of God to save his own people even before they were born.

The Old Testament, with its story of God's people, holy laws, covenant, true prophets, priests and kings, leads in one direction: *the kingdom of God will come!* Yet when the Messiah Jesus came to the holy city of Jerusalem, the authorities plotted his execution. Jesus knew what was coming his way and the terrible judgement that would follow. We read:

> *When the city came into view, he wept over it. "If you had only recognised this day, and everything that was good for you! But now it's too late. In the days ahead your enemies are going to bring up their heavy artillery and surround you, pressing in from every side. They'll smash you and your babies on the pavement. Not one stone will be left intact. All this because you didn't recognise and welcome God's personal visit."*
>
> Luke 19:41-44 (MSG)

It took God's only Son to make that incredible journey of rejection, suffering and death. He was born to die. He leads and points the road to the Father. He and he alone is the *way,* the *truth* and the *life*[33] – not by some political scheme or social agenda but *only* by making and finishing that incredible journey to the *cross.*[34]

Can you see yourself fitting into any of the four categories of public response to Jesus? If so, which one? He came then. He comes now. He will come again. Welcome our coming King Jesus!

Let us take up the challenge as never before to reach the lost with the message of Christ.

Let us not be hesitant to face people with the coming judgement and the need for repentance and receiving Christ, who alone is the only hope of life and glory to come.

Let us be sure to join him in his incredible journey – he to save, us to tell – so that others will join us in a chorus of praise and worship:

> *'Blessed is the king who comes*
> *in the name of the Lord!'*
> *'Peace in heaven and glory in the highest!'*
>
> Luke 19:38 (NIVUK)

---

[33] See John 14:6
[34] See Ephesians 2:16; Hebrews 12:2; Philemon 3:18; Matthew 10:38; Mark 8:34

QUESTIONS

What significant factors stand out for you about Jesus' last journey to Jerusalem before his execution?

Many in society today have turned away from God to pursue their take on life. Given the urgency of the message, what should the Christian do to reach them with the gospel?

Why do you think most religious leaders were so strongly opposed to Jesus' entry into Jerusalem while the public majority were bowled over with excitement?

9

What is Meant by the Blood of the Lamb?

This is the kind of life you've been invited into, the kind of life Christ lived. He suffered everything that came his way so you would know that it could be done, and also know how to do it, step-by-step.

1 Peter 2:21 (MSG)

NEXT, OUR JOURNEY FOCUSES ON THE VERY heart of Christendom: the cross of Christ. I invite you to examine with me the basics and significance of sacrificial blood in the Bible in general and the shed blood of God's Son Jesus in particular.

In the year 2000 my wife Helen and I were privileged to be sent to Atlanta as delegates to the International Congress held there. John Gowans had only just been elected as the 16th General of The Salvation Army and was the leader of the congress. His sermon was unforgettable. He preached with passionate appeal to that huge congregation, launched into his talk with these words: 'Are you washed in the blood of the Lamb?' We don't hear so much of that phrase these days, and rarely sing those words.

We were serving in Africa when our home church in central Scotland featured the musical *The Blood of the Lamb*. Far from home, the news of the success of that musical reached us. People from all over attended each night and the message of the redemptive work of the Lord Jesus Christ was propelled through the music and lyrics of that production.

The script by John Gowans, with music by John Larsson, depicts how people from all walks of life and from every level of society came to know the power of the cleansing blood of the Lord Jesus Christ and as such were transformed eternally. The musical itself was a means of great blessing both to those who participated and those who attended. There are different ways that God uses to get his great message of salvation to his people. I wonder, is it time for another Christian musical where you are?

The Bible speaks of the holy significance of blood and sacrifice as a means of forgiveness and saving. It was the blood of a lamb smeared on the door frames of Hebrew homes that saved them from the destroyer angel sent by God. By contrast, the Egyptians' firstborn and livestock with no 'Passover sacrifice' symbol to God were killed.[35] Fast forward to the Tabernacle and later Temple sacrificial ceremonies where the priest placed his hands upon a pure, healthy animal before sacrificing it. The act symbolised the transference of the sins of the people onto the innocent creature, as a gesture of God's forgiveness.[36] These his-

---

[35] See Exodus 12:21-27
[36] See Leviticus 1:1-4

torical events were a precursor to the crowning prophecy of Christ spelt out for us in Isaiah where we read:

> *...he was pierced for our rebellion,*
> *crushed for our sins*
> *...the Lord laid on him*
> *the sins of us all...*
>
> *Isaiah 53:5,6 (NLT)*

This same message of the sacrificial lamb is proclaimed by John the Baptist who, on meeting Jesus at the start of his mission of God's kingdom, cries out, 'Look, the Lamb of God, who takes away the sin of the world!'[37] Peter elaborates even further: '"He himself bore our sins" in his body on the cross, so that we might die to sin and live for righteousness; "by his wounds you have been healed."'[38] Paul puts it this way: '[He] gave himself to rescue us from the present evil age, according to the will of our God and father...'[39] John paints a vivid picture: 'Carrying his own cross, he went out to the place of the skull (which in Aramaic is called Golgotha). There they crucified him...'[40] On that day, the Lamb of God was slain for all mankind!

Once the power of the blood of Christ touches us, we can't ever be the same again. In 1 John 1 we are urged simply and profoundly to walk in the light of God.

> *But if we walk in the light, God himself being*
> *the light, we also experience a shared life with*

---

[37] John 1:29 (NIVUK)
[38] 1 Peter 2:24 (NIVUK)
[39] Galatians 1:4,5 (NIVUK)
[40] John 19:17,18 (NIVUK)

> *one another, as the sacrificed blood of Jesus,*
> *God's Son, purges all our sin.*
>
> *1 John 1:7 (MSG)*

Unpack this and you have the blood of the Lamb linked to the life of holiness. There it is, clear as crystal: if we walk in the light, God has set in motion his provision to purify us from whatever sin would mar our fellowship with him and each other. Someone has said, 'Participation in Christ's blood is participation in his life...' When you experience the effects of the cleansing blood of Christ it means you're living a transparent and transformed life. Nothing to hide, everything to shout about!

QUESTIONS

Besides musicals, what other ways do you think would be effective in reaching people with the gospel?

What is the connection between sin, suffering, salvation and sanctification?

Evaluating the scriptural texts here, what do they have to say about the significance of the 'blood of the Lamb'?

10

What does the Blood Say Today?

*If we claim to be without sin, we deceive
ourselves and the truth is not in us. If we confess
our sins, he is faithful and just and will forgive
us our sins and purify us from all
unrighteousness.*

1 John 1:8,9 (NIVUK)

IN 1 JOHN 1:5-10, THE APOSTLE CONTRASTS
light with darkness and sin with forgiveness. Part of this
darkness is 'false claims' by those who deliberately place
'light' and 'darkness' practices in the same mould. It was a
heresy known as Manichaeism (a gnostic religion). They
regarded the body as a blanket covering the human spirit.
The idea was, you can defile and do as you like with your
body while at the same time your inner self will still be
pure and holy. The apostle John condemned this practice
outright as heresy put out there by those bent on denying
that sin breaks fellowship with God.

In today's world aspects of this still occur. Some claim
they have fellowship with God and believe they can be
holy, yet neglect to go to the cross of Christ for cleansing
and forgiveness. Others lay claim to mystical intimacy
with God but, in truth, still walk in darkness!

Today's church, as always, has to deal with those who
think we should keep our religious views private. We have

in the universal Church many who mind their P's and Q's in fear that they might be singled out for ridicule. The truth is, more and more are acquiescing and now 'play the game' as an easy option (although, to be fair, some would rather not sign up to popular practice). Is there a way out and a way forward? Yes, indeed there is – but space must first be given to the cause before applying the cure.

The very word 'sin' has melted from everyday speech and the big search is on to 'fix it' by multiple schemes – scientific, psychological and social. While these disciplines are not without merit, they often ignore or are ignorant of the invasion of sin on the planet and in every person. Many are blind and deaf to who God is or what he commands. Others laugh at his laws on 'living and forgiving' and deride his offer of salvation.

Those washed in the blood of the Lamb have this great plus in their day-to-day living. It is nothing less than the power of the blood of the Lamb of God. It imparts within a heavenly strength that shapes how the people of God face the challenges of today. It is this cleansing power of the blood of the Lamb that energises, empowers and enables the believer to live a life of holiness.

What shape does the life of holiness take in today's world? Quite simply, it boils down to the believer's response to the Holy Spirit; how we act, think, speak, feel. It is a challenging matter of how we live out the faith: how we treat our nearest and dearest; how we behave when no one can see us. The art of holiness is where God comes first and each person is invited to mirror his love and beauty. To know him is to love him and to 'live him'.

To be like Jesus, this hope possesses me,
In every thought and deed,
This is my aim my creed...
His Spirit helping me,
Like him I'll be.[41]

The only way to live a life of holiness is to be like Jesus. John writes:

> *...when Christ is openly revealed, we'll see him*
> *– and in seeing him, become like him ... with*
> *the glistening purity of Jesus' life as a model for*
> *our own.*
>
> *1 John 3:2b,3 (MSG)*

Such likeness, begun now, will be complete!

At the end of the musical *Blood of the Lamb,* the cast are assembled in the waiting area before entering Heaven wearing earthly clothing. Next, they pass through the veil from death to life in 'the glory' where they look on the indescribable splendour of the Risen Conquering Lamb. Finally, they emerge in dazzling robes of white!

> *After this I looked, and there before me was a*
> *great multitude that no one could count, from*
> *every nation, tribe, people and language,*
> *standing before the throne and before the Lamb*
> *... wearing white robes ... all worshipping God*
> *... Then one ... asked ... 'These in white robes-*
> *who are they, and where did they come from?'*
> *I answered, 'Sir, you know.' And he said, 'These*

---

[41] *To Be Like Jesus;* John Gowans (1934-2012)

*are they who have come out of great
tribulation; they have washed their robes and
made them white in the blood of the Lamb.'*

Revelation 7:9-14 (NIVUK)

The cross of Christ – his shed blood, the way of life
opened wide – brings all face to face with an inescapable
question, one with an answer only you can provide: are
you washed in the blood of the Lamb?

QUESTIONS

For the Christian, has 'political correctness' gone too far?
Do we 'go with the flow' to the extent of compromising
foundational truths of the gospel? Give some examples.

_____

_____

_____

_____

_____

'To know Christ is to love him and to live for him.' With
this statement in mind, describe how a life of holiness
looks in today's world.

_____

_____

_____

_____

_____

_____

_____

11

Seeing Christ

John 20:11-18

*Then Jesus told him, 'Because you have seen
me, you have believed; blessed are those who
have not seen and yet have believed.'*

John 20:29 (NIVUK)

A SPACIOUS GARDEN AND A SAFE HOUSE WERE
the setting for Jesus' resurrection appearances. The
Gospels record he appeared only to believers. First to see
him was a woman, Mary Magdalene, a former prostitute
made whole by Jesus. The other disciples, including John,
Peter and Thomas, encountered him 'behind locked doors,
because they were afraid of the Jewish authorities'[42].

In the dark, Mary, distressed by the crucifixion, made
her way to the tomb where Jesus' body had been laid. To
her horror she found it empty. She ran for Peter and John,
who raced to the scene. They found the folded grave
clothes as if the body of Jesus had simply evaporated out
of them. Peter left in shock. John, the disciple who had
been so close to Jesus, rejected any notion that the body
had been stolen. Instead, though he had not seen, he
believed that God had raised Jesus to life.

---

[42] John 20:19 (GNB)

John is recorded as the first of those who who 'saw and believed'[43] even though, unlike Mary, at this point he hadn't yet seen Jesus in his resurrected form.[44] R.V.G. Tasker writes:

> ...*without having any encounter with the risen Lord, he believed that the Lord's body had not been removed by human hands, but raised by divine intervention.*[45]

Frankly, it is right to say he was the first of millions ever since of whom Jesus says, 'Blessed are those who believe without seeing me.'[46]

Alone by the tomb, Mary cried inconsolably. 'Woman, why are you crying?'[47] asked two angels. Later Mary heard the same question; this time she had no idea it was Jesus himself who was asking it. Perhaps tears blurred her vision, or it might have been that she was facing the empty tomb and Jesus was standing behind her. Either way, when she heard her name spoken – 'Mary' – she knew it was her Lord. Can you imagine her joy? Jesus, crucified and dead, alive here and standing in front of her! Not able to hold herself back, she threw herself at Jesus. 'Do not hold on to me, for I have not yet ascended to the Father,'[48] Jesus said.

---

[43] John 20:8 (NIVUK)

[44] See verse 8

[45] R.V.G. Tasker; *Tyndale NT Commentaries;* Inter-Varsity Press (1968)

[46] Verse 29

[47] John 20:15 (NIVUK)

[48] John 20:17 (NIVUK)

He then told her to go and tell the others. What news Mary brought to the disciples that day: 'I have seen the Lord!'[49]

Centuries later, we see Christ through the eyes of faith. The Holy Spirit makes him known to us. We experience him within our lives in a way that was impossible when he walked this earth. May our response always be to go and tell others of our walk with Jesus. After all, 'We know these things are true by believing, not by seeing.'[50]

---

[49] John 20:18 (ESV)
[50] 2 Corinthians 5:7 (NLT)

QUESTIONS

That old adage 'seeing is believing' would fit the bill for so many today (or so they think) as grounds for belief. As a Christian, what advice would you offer that would help such people to believe?

Mary Magdalene plays a pivotal role in her encounter with the risen Saviour. In your own words, write a simple account of this and apply it to today's world.

Here, as in many other parts of the Bible, angels appear as messengers with a special task to carry out. Why do you think angels appeared to Mary and what do they mean to you?

12

Only Believe

John 20:19-31

Thomas said to him, 'My Lord and my God!'

John 20:28 (NIVUK)

IT WAS IN THE EVENING THAT JESUS APPEARED to his frightened disciples saying, 'Peace be with you!'[51] At the sight of the master, they were beside themselves with joy. He showed them his wounded hands and side saying, 'As the Father has sent me, I am sending you.'[52] Jesus then gifted his disciples with the Holy Spirit and his power to proclaim the message of forgiveness of sins.

Thomas was not present when all this happened, and when told later, 'We have seen the Lord!'[53] he was sceptical. He insisted on seeing for himself before he would believe. A week later, as the group gathered, Jesus reappeared and invited Thomas to believe by touching his wounds. He didn't. Instead he confessed, 'My Lord and my God!'[54]

---

[51] John 20:26 (NIV)
[52] John 20:21 (NIV)
[53] John 20:25 (NIV)
[54] John 20:28 (NIV)

This is the first time Jesus is called 'God' and it's from the lips of one plagued with doubts. In search of truth, doubt is not an enemy. It can be our ally to achieve a certainty that the unthinking and unquestioning can never know. All of us at some time in our lives will pass through a season of doubt.

Times of loss, spiritual dryness, disillusionment, despair and circumstances over which we have no control, can rob us of our confidence in God. That said, we should never confuse doubt with failure nor carry the burden of guilt. We often see ourselves mirrored in Thomas, but we do not find in Jesus judgement and condemnation, but rather a tenderness that in the end will lead us deeper into faith without sight.

QUESTIONS

What do you make of Thomas's struggle to believe on Christ's resurrection unless he can see and touch his wounds? How can we help those who hold a similar view to Thomas's?

How should Christians deal with doubt in their journey of faith?

What are your thoughts on Thomas when he called Jesus 'God'?

13

Amazing Encounter

John 21:1-14

'It is the Lord!'

John 21:7 (NIVUK)

WHEN THE ONE WE LOVE MOST IN THE WORLD
is gone and when cherished dreams turn to ashes, what
then? Somehow most find a way to go on. With the
crucifixion of Jesus, hope died for the disciples. Three
years earlier, at the start of Jesus' mission, things had been
so promising. There was the unforgettable dawn on the
same shores of Galilee when, after a night of failure to find
fish, Jesus had directed them to an enormous haul. More
than just performing a miracle of finding fish, he had told
Peter, '...From now on you'll be fishing for men and
women...'[55] Then each one '...left everything and followed
him'[56]. What a promise it had been back then – but what
of now? With Jesus gone, a cruel darkness closed in.

Here, once again, the scene is set. After a fruitless night
of fishing they spotted a stranger on the shore who called
out to them, 'Throw your net on the right side of the boat
and you'll find some.' They did exactly that. Result: the

---

[55] Luke 5:1-10 (MSG)
[56] Luke 5:11 (NIVUK)

catch of a lifetime! The greatest lesson we can learn is to follow the commands of Christ; when we do, we discover riches of God in abundance!

John shouted, 'It is the Lord!' Instantly Peter plunged into the sea and at top speed made for his risen master. Hearts racing with excitement, the others followed in the boat, dragging the nets bulging with fish. A small fire crackled with the smell of cooking; Jesus had prepared a meal. 'Come and have breakfast,' he called and, typically, served them all. Here we have it: Jesus, the Bread of Life, giving himself in service, word and love. Imagine dining with the Son of God!

It's not as far-fetched as it might seem. We are all invited to come and share fellowship with the Lord of Life himself. Still today, he journeys with us along the shoreline of tragedy, disappointment and failure. His hand reaches out to the needy and neglected. He speaks still to the hopeless and despairing. He does so through people like you and me who have heard his call in the night and follow where he leads. And, as far as dreams go, he transforms us so that we long for the things that please God.

Why not read both Luke 5:1-11 and Matthew 4:18-22? The narrative in each is visual and takes you on a journey into a gripping, challenging and inspiring atmosphere.

QUESTIONS

When Peter was first called to follow Jesus and then called a second time, lost fish (men and women) were found by him obeying Jesus' command. How important is it in our walk with Jesus to follow where he leads?

Imagine hearing Jesus say to you, 'Come and have breakfast.' Think of it; he's chief, host and provider. What would you do? How would you feel? Whom would you like to invite? How would you reach others with the news? Who most needs to come?

Based on the lessons drawn from this chapter, how might a Christian approach people in their neighbourhood who find themselves burdened with great sorrow and loss?

14

How Can We See Jesus?

John 1:18; 14:9; Colossians 2:3; 1:15-20

Christ is the visible image of the invisible God.
Colossians 1:15 (NLT)

THE OLD ADAGE 'FAITH IS BLIND' CAN BE DECEIV-ing. What do you think? In the Christian faith, the statement 'seeing is believing' is turned on its head so that 'believing is seeing'. Faith is the catalyst of sight. And what a picture it presents!

How are we to see God? Let's begin by focusing on the Son. Some readers will remember Robert Powell's portrayal of Jesus in Zeffirelli's film, *Jesus of Nazareth*. Does this help us see what Jesus might have looked like? Or what do you make of those who have attempted to reconstruct the face of Jesus using first-century skulls as a model? Some may remember BBC TV's *Son of God* series presented by Jeremy Bowen, in which this very matter was looked at.

In the year 2000, the UK featured many memorable activities and exhibitions. I was thrilled to have visited the *Seeing Salvation* exhibition held at London's National Gallery; a wide variety of impressions of Christ were displayed there, painted by artists through the centuries – each an attempt to capture on canvas the real Christ. The record attendances surely suggested not only an appreciation of art and religion, prompted by a curiosity that wants to 'see', but also a searching, driven by the desire to find deeper meaning and purpose to life.

Above my desk I had for some time a photocopy of the painting *Christ in Majesty*. Taken from a fourth-century mural, this has the first and last letters of the Greek alphabet, alpha and omega, flanking the image of Christ. While I treasure these works of art, I have to ask, should we focus on such works to see the One hidden from our eyes? The short answer, I believe, is no – for two reasons. Firstly, image is no substitute for reality, however much the likeness. The family snapshot or selfie is no substitute for the real person, cute as it may be. Secondly, even were we in possession of a true image of Jesus, some would soon see it as an object of worship. The apostle Paul says:

> *So, my dear friends, flee from the worship of idols.*
>
> *1 Corinthians 10:14 (NLT)*

What then are we to make of the apostle John when he writes, 'No one has ever seen God'[57]? Jesus said, 'Anyone who has seen me has seen the Father.'[58] There you have it; to see God we must look on Jesus. He and no other unveils to us God's face. Look on Christ the Son and you see God. Jesus' earthly ministry shows us what God is like.

In his letter to the church at Colossae, Paul refutes the twisted thinking over Christ's status from Jewish legalism and humanistic philosophy. Each fails to take Christ

---

[57] John 1:18 (NIVUK)
[58] John 14:9 (NIVUK)

seriously and plays him down, preferring strict Jewish ceremonial or ascetic practices to the claims of the Messiah – insisting upon the possession of secret and magical knowledge as the key to superior spiritual life. This is nothing short of heresy. *No,* says Paul to all of that. In Christ 'are hidden all the treasures of wisdom and knowledge'[59]. Christ is sufficient and supreme. He alone is, and must be, number one.

I have a book entitled *100 Great Lives* in which Jesus is depicted only as a prophet, miracle worker and teacher. He is not believed to be God's Son. The fact remains, Judaism clings to this same stance, while Jehovah's Witnesses see him as one whose life began in heaven and that he is a separate entity, so that he is not part of the Trinity. Mormonism falls short of recognition of Christ as truly God and truly man. Islam, in turn, rejects the divinity of Christ wholesale. For each of these listed faiths, the triune God (the Trinity) as 'undivided in essence and co-equal in power and glory' is a non-starter. Each fails to accord to Christ his divine status. Yet, according to the New Testament, Jesus is the very glory of God revealed. The apostle Paul pulls no punches and says it as God the Holy Spirit has inspired him to do:

> *The Son is the image of the invisible God, the firstborn over all creation. For in him all things were created: things in heaven and on earth, visible and invisible, whether thrones or powers or rulers or authorities; all things have been created through him and for him. He is before*

---

[59] Colossians 2:3 (NIVUK)

> *all things, and in him all things hold together.*
> *And he is the head of the body, the church; he*
> *is the beginning and the firstborn from among*
> *the dead, so that in everything he might have*
> *the supremacy. For God was pleased to have <u>all</u>*
> *<u>his fullness</u> dwell in him, and through him to*
> *reconcile to himself all things, whether things*
> *on earth or things in heaven, by making peace*
> *through his blood, shed on the cross.*
>
> Colossians 1:15-20 (NIVUK, emphasis added)

By 'fullness' Paul is saying that Christ is filled, or 'jam-packed', overflowing with God. Full divinity is in the man Jesus, without the least suggestion that he is anyone else. We have here one God only, who in all his fullness dwells in his Son. '...everything of God finds its proper place in him without crowding'[60] is how The Message Bible puts it. Because of his divine identity he has pre-eminence over all things. You can read more about this in Philippians 2:6-11.

Let no one treat Christ lightly. God the Father has given all rights of creation, salvation and sovereignty into the hands of his Son. God's very character is in Jesus. The apostle John adds:

> *The Word became flesh and made his dwelling*
> *among us. We have seen his glory, the glory of*
> *the one and only Son, who came from the*
> *Father, full of grace and truth.*
>
> John 1:14 (NIVUK)

---

[60] Colossians 1:18 (MSG)

In short, though distinct from God, Christ is not different from him. Though distinguishable from the Father, he is God! This is what Christians believe – *one* God, not three.

QUESTIONS

How crucial is it for a Christian to believe that in Jesus, the divine and human natures are united so that he is truly and properly God and truly and properly man?

John 1 declares that Jesus is an inseparable part of the Godhead. Verse 18 (NIV) reads, 'No one has ever seen God, but the one and only Son, who is himself God and is in closest relationship with the Father...' Other faiths and substitutes for Christianity disagree with the New Testament's declaration here. What do you have to say in defence of Jesus' God-status?

When a person worships something or someone other than God, it is idolatry. List and comment on a range of idolatrous acts that are commonplace in our world today. Why is idolatry dangerous and destructive?

15

Love Conquers All

John 21:15-25

'Do you love me? ... Follow me!'
John 21:17,19 (NIVUK)

FROM THE HEAVENLY JOY OF THE ENCOUNTER between the disciples and the risen Christ on the shores of Galilee, Jesus takes Peter to one side, asking, '...do you love me more than these?'[61] Except for the 'more than these', Jesus had repeated the love question two more times. Previously at Jesus' trial, Peter had fallen apart and hastily given up on his promise to stand by his Lord to the death, if needs be. Scared and worried for his own skin, he had denied three times that he knew Jesus. Can we blame him? By going over painful ground, was Jesus being vindictive and unforgiving? No. Any good counsellor takes us back to issues of the past, however painful, to face them. By this route, healing can take place.

What were the 'these' Jesus referred to here? It may have been his work, his friends and family. However dear, they must take second place to Christ. This way, past failures can be faced, repented of and the course set for a

---

[61] John 21:15 (NIVUK)

new future. When we follow Christ no one and nothing can fill his place. Isaac Watts expressed it this way:

> *Love so amazing, so divine,*
> *Demands my soul, my life, my all.*[62]

Peter's denial was being swallowed up by the incredible love Christ held for him. The love tie was to enable him, with all his weakness, to serve God's people. He was to feed and shepherd old and young alike after Jesus was finally to leave them, returning to his Father God. When Jesus said to Peter, 'Follow me!' he knew that for Peter, following would culminate in a martyr's death. Tradition has it he suffered death by crucifixion. The forgiven denier could now face the future knowing he truly loved Christ his master above everyone and everything and that his Lord loved him beyond words.

Our following Christ may not require such levels of sacrifice. When Peter saw John approach, he asked, 'Master, what's going to happen to him?'[63] Jesus responded sharply, '...what's that to you?'[64] In the end John lived to be a very old man; Peter did not. In different ways Christ calls us to serve him as he has planned. All we need to know is that, renewed in Christ, his love conquers all!

Even our noblest aspirations for the kingdom can take a beating. Pledges to be reliable and faithful can suffer a

---

[62] *Amazing Grace;* Isaac Watts
[63] John 21:21 (MSG)
[64] John 21:22 (MSG)

setback. Still, Jesus stands by us. Why not take a little time to look at Luke 22:31-34;54-62?

QUESTIONS

What do you think was going on when Jesus asked Peter three times if he loved him? Did Jesus' question have a past and future relevance; if so, what was that?

_____

_____

_____

_____

Failure and loss from the past must be faced squarely before healing can come. Is there something in your life that has broken you? Someone you can't forgive? What do you think God would have you do?

_____

_____

_____

_____

What did Jesus do for Peter that brought healing?

_____

_____

_____

16

Blue Sky Message

Acts 1:1-11; Ephesians 1:15-22

"But you will receive power when the Holy Spirit comes upon you. And you will be my witnesses ... to the ends of the earth."

Acts 1:8 (NLT)

JESUS' LIFE, DEATH AND RESURRECTION ARE characterised by God's power and presence. Christ's ascension comes after forty days during which, in his resurrection form, he has shared meals and conversations with his disciples. But then he must leave them so that the Spirit may come.

Jesus instructs his disciples to go to Jerusalem and wait for God's gift: the Holy Spirit. Receiving a farewell blessing from their master, they stand spellbound as he is taken into the clouds. The startling appearance of two men dressed in white guarantees their undivided attention. These men gently rebuke the disciples:

"Why do you just stand here looking up at an empty sky? This very Jesus was taken up from among you to heaven will come as certainly – and mysteriously – as he left."

Acts 1:9-11 (MSG)

The Ascension marks the conclusion of Christ's earthly ministry and focuses on the promised Holy Spirit power and presence until Christ returns. The Spirit coming in power will make known the glory of Christ's death and resurrection. Jesus had instructed his disciples, 'Do not leave Jerusalem, but wait for the gift my Father promised.'[65] Ten days later that promise was fulfilled. Pentecost came with a torrent of transforming power! The truth regarding Jesus as the Son of God was now lifted from its limited domain and revealed to many.

What the disciples experienced in those few short years with Jesus was truly amazing. However, even after their master's death and resurrection, they had still not grasped the real significance of his life and work. After being instructed to wait for the coming of the Spirit, they asked, 'Lord, are you at that time going to restore the kingdom to Israel?'[66] They were to learn that the kingdom of God was not defined by some narrow political agenda, however sound or just. God was in the business of changing lives that would in turn change the world! God's rule comes when God's people are empowered by his Spirit.

The church today must not repeat the mistake the disciples made in seeking to make a better world with the world's tools. Followers of Christ do not try to bend their leader to their agenda. On the contrary, issues impacting people's lives, whether political, social, domestic, economic, moral or otherwise, must be submitted to the lead which 'comes from above'[67]. When the Holy Spirit

---

[65] Acts 1:4 (NIVUK)
[66] Acts 1:6 (NIVUK)
[67] John 3:31 (NIVUK)

comes to those who wait, he brings wisdom, enlightenment and the *same* strength that raised Christ from the dead! The power of God's presence is manifested perfectly in Jesus.

We need to exercise care that we do not lose sight of our identity in Christ and the fact that he is in a unique category. He alone has authority. The ascension of Jesus – like his birth, death and resurrection – bears witness to that authority. Christ alone is 'the way and the truth and the life'[68].

The world's perception of power is, at its simplest, the power to do anything. The world we all know is in trouble, big time! The abuser in the home, the knife-carrier in the street, the secret lover, the stranger to the truth or the one who tramples over the feelings of others to 'get on' – each of these speak of disregarding the freedom and dignity of fellow human beings who, too, are made in the image of God.

There is another power, one which Jesus told his disciples to wait for, pray for and yearn for. It is the power of the Holy Spirit. It is not natural. Nor is it innate or automatic. It cannot be acquired even by the most disciplined moral standards. It is not to be found in philosophy or even a theology. It is, as Jesus said, a *gift* from God. This and only this is the power that will make all things new: new people, new relationships and a new world.

It is the power of the Holy Spirit, who brings Jesus into focus and through whom we see God. It is by that power

---

[68] John 14:6 (NIVUK)

that the disciples lived to God's glory and witnessed to the world. It is clear from God's Word that the disciples experienced such a baptism of the Holy Spirit at Pentecost that they turned the world upside down. Today, we, like them, are commanded to wait and pray for that same baptism, then to go into every avenue of life with the greatest message the world can ever know!

QUESTIONS

Prior to and just after the Ascension of Jesus, what words, actions and events do you see as significant in the life of the Church?

Who is the Holy Spirit in relation to Jesus and God? What does the Holy Spirit do in/for the life of the believer? Can the Church function without the Holy Spirit; if not, why not?

Compare and contrast the world's perception of power to that of God's Holy Spirit?

Prayer

Lord, thank you for giving yourself to us without reserve!

Teach us to follow your example. Grant us your grace that we also may give ourselves away to others and see you in all.

Amen.

Contact the Author

To contact the author, please write to:

Jim Bryden
c/o Onwards and Upwards Publishers Ltd.
4 The Old Smithy
London Road
Rockbeare
Exeter
EX5 2EA

Or send an email to:

jamesandhelenbryden@icloud.com

More information about the author can be found
on the book's web page:

www.onwardsandupwards.org/journey-of-faith-messiah-jesus

What Shall I Read Next?

This book opens up Paul's letter to the Ephesians, with twenty-one daily readings, explanations and applications, as well as optional short exercises to help you dig deeper into the Word.

ISBN: 978-1-78815-717-9
RRP: £6.99

Learn more about God's plan to reach the world through the church, the Body of Christ. Jim shows how believers are called to live out their lives and share the gospel with perseverance and faithfulness, with the promise of a heavenly reward.

ISBN: 978-1-78815-557-1
RRP: £6.99